Praise for *Christmas Traditions*

It's so easy to get caught up in the busyness of the Christmas season and lose sight of the significance of the *why*. These helpful Advent devotions will guide your whole family in drawing spiritual applications from the familiar objects, sights, and sounds that fill the holiday.

—Jim Daly, president, Focus on the Family

Marissa & Miriam Barbee have crafted a most wonderful & creative Advent book, designed to connect holiday traditions (many of them of pagan origins) to the biblical truths that flow naturally and relevantly from them. This fine devotional is a perfect tool for Christian families wanting to enhance their appreciation of the Christmas season. I highly recommend it!

—Reverend Ed Tafilowski, Foothills Fellowship, in Littleton, Colorado

Christmas
TRADITIONS

Christmas

TRADITIONS

Through the Lens of Scripture

AN ADVENT BOOK

Marissa Barbee

Published by Redemption Press, PO Box 427, Enumclaw, WA 98022.
Toll-Free (844) 2REDEEM (273-3336)

Redemption Press is honored to present this title in partnership with the author. The views expressed or implied in this work are those of the author. Redemption Press provides our imprint seal representing design excellence, creative content, and high-quality production.

The author has tried to recreate events, locales, and conversations from memories of them. In order to maintain their anonymity, in some instances the names of individuals, some identifying characteristics, and some details may have been changed, such as physical properties, occupations, and places of residence.

Unless otherwise indicated, all Scripture quotations are from The Holy Bible, English Standard Version ® (ESV®), copyright © 2001 by Crossway, a publishing ministry of Good News Publishers. Used by permission. All rights reserved.

Scripture taken from the New King James Version®. Copyright © 1982 by Thomas Nelson. Used by permission. All rights reserved.

ISBN 13: 978-1-64645-649-9 (Hardback)
978-1-64645-549-2 (ePub)
978-1-64645-548-5 (Mobi)

Library of Congress Catalog Card Number: 2021921267

Dedication

This book is dedicated to
Miriam, Joseph, Joel, Hannah, Avram, Aaron, Jonathan, Avigail, and Sharon—
you are my reason!

Foreword

It was a normal Sunday morning during the summer of 2019 when a new family entered the worship center of our church. New visitors are always a joyous sight, as it is the heart of our church leadership and members to help new attendees find a good church home. As the family of God, we love new families! That being true, this new family specifically caught the eye of many that Sunday morning and during subsequent worship services. A family of eleven can certainly cause anyone to pause and count—and count again! The Barbee family filled multiple rows as Scott and Marissa gracefully ushered in their nine beautiful children, from high school teens all the way down to a ridiculously cute toddler. This well-dressed, well-mannered, kind-hearted family made an immediate mark and impact on our congregation.

Since that first encounter, it has been a true pleasure getting to know the Barbee family, and I'm thankful to the Lord that I can call them friends. More than that, they are colaborers in Christ as we all seek to know God more and make him known to the world around us. Scott has been faithful to use his seminary training and his gifts of teaching and preaching to help grow our congregation in God's Word. Many of the high school and middle school children have lived out their faith in Christ by loving God's people through various areas of service within the church. The Barbee family is a huge blessing to many!

That brings me to Marissa, the author of the book you are about to enjoy. If anyone has the right to look upon their family and say with confidence, "*This* is my ministry!" it would be Marissa Barbee. A loving and faithful wife, a 24/7 keeper of the home, and a homeschooling mother of nine amazing children is a God-given ministry that requires all the strength and energy that one can receive from the Lord. And yet, in the midst of all this, Marissa has now added the title of "author" to her repertoire. Not only that, but her eldest child, Miriam, has partnered with her mother as illustrator of this book. A family labor of love to be sure!

Marissa faithfully dedicates her time investing into her family spiritually, educationally, and relationally. This book on Christmas traditions, as viewed through the lens of Scripture, is simply an outflow of the work that she does day in and day out as a loving wife and mother. Training our children in the Word of God while "competing" with worldly messaging and influences can seem like a daunting task. However, as believers in Christ, we are commanded to persevere in the midst of adversity, rely on the power of the Holy Spirit, and to have a biblical worldview as we engage with various aspects of life. Marissa has done this well in helping her family understand Christmas traditions in light of the centerpiece of the holiday—Jesus Christ. Thankfully, she now shares her wisdom and insight with the rest of us in the pages of this book.

Christmas is a very unique and special time of year when Christians celebrate the birth of our Savior in many tangible ways. As a pastor, teacher, husband, and father of two, I can attest to the fact that Christmas is one of the most wondrous and joy-filled times of the year. Various traditions, whether cultural or passed down by our families, come alive this time of year—all with the purpose of pointing us to Christ.

At times, if we're honest, we find ourselves lost in the hustle and bustle of the season, surrounded by many beautiful reminders of why we are celebrating but running too fast to remember and reflect on the *reason for the season: Jesus Christ.* Christmas colors, décor, music, food, stories, and family traditions can begin to fall prey to consumerism, entertainment, and stressed-filled obligations. In light of this, we all need some help at times pressing pause, reflecting on the purpose of the incarnation of Christ, and learning not just to celebrate a national holiday but to worship a holy God who sent his Son to save our souls. This is the most beautiful gift of all.

To that end, Marissa (with the artistic help of her daughter Miriam) has skillfully and prayerfully taken the well-known aspects of family Christmas celebrations and woven them into daily conversations about what is truly important in life. The Advent devotions found in this book will help families gather together again in the awe and wonder of our Savior, while redeeming the familiar traditions which may have faded into the common noise of a busy season. The thoughtful connections and beautiful illustrations will give every reader a new appreciation for time-honored traditions and will also provide a means to grow in the grace and knowledge of our Lord and Savior, Jesus Christ.

It is with much appreciation to Marissa and her family, and with great expectation of how God might speak through the following pages, that I commend this book to you and your family. May the Lord bring a time of refreshment as you ponder the birth of Jesus. He is most certainly our Wonderful Counselor, Mighty God, Everlasting Father, and the Prince of Peace.

Mike Hartle, Lead Pastor
Black Forest Chapel
Colorado Springs, Colorado

Acknowledgments

First and foremost, I thank Jesus Christ for being my Savior. Without his sacrifice, his saving grace, and his unending love, there would be no message to share. May he be glorified!

Roger and Mary Lynn Twombly, thank you for being the builders of my foundation. In your faithfulness and intention in raising us in the Christian faith, you were able to strike a balance between the fun and the lesson . . . truly laying the foundations for my life and this book.

Susan Mabey, thank you for being my inspiration. You are still my favorite storyteller. Your reading of the story of the candy cane's origins so many years ago captivated me, gave me a passion for connecting the everyday to spiritual lessons, and now lives on in this book to reach many others.

Jerry Barbee, thank you for being my visionary—the first to see and share with me what you thought this could become. What you envisioned nine years ago has come to fruition.

Mike Hartle, thank you for giving this project a jump start. This book would likely not have moved beyond its infancy without your request to make it available to a broader audience.

Miriam Barbee, thank you for investing in the project as my illustrator. It was such a joy to work side by side on it with you. I appreciate your talent and ability to take my vision, improve upon it with your variety of styles, and bring life to each lesson.

Anita Johnson, my encourager, thank you for coming alongside me in this journey, sharing abundant joy, talent, and experience. Your skill and insight as you applied the red pen to the very first draft were immensely helpful. Your faith in me and in the value of what I had written were a huge blessing.

Liz Harper, thank you for being my pathfinder. The experiences, lessons learned, and encouragement you shared as another first-time author were invaluable.

Thank you to Redemption Press and my entire publishing team. You have been an enormous blessing: challenging me to dig deeper, helping me to express the message more clearly, encouraging and guiding me through the process, and handling all the behind-the-scenes issues that so overwhelmed me at the beginning of this process. You each were instrumental in nurturing this project to maturity.

Scott Barbee, my partner in life, thank you for also being my partner in this project. You were my strength, my encourager, my theology coach, and my spotter who was right there to offer the kind of help needed whenever the burden seemed too heavy to lift on my own.

Prologue

Looking for the Savior

You shall teach them diligently to your children, and shall talk of them when you sit in your house, and when you walk by the way, and when you lie down, and when you rise.

Deuteronomy 6:7

Many Christians look down upon the "pagan roots" of Christmas. Maybe rightly so. After all, we want to avoid watering down our faith or worshipping anything but the one true God. On the other hand, the traditional symbols of those roots are pervasive enough to be unavoidable, so it makes sense to put them to use in drawing our children to Christ.

Advent is a time for families to ponder God's plan of salvation. The essence of that plan is Christ's coming to the world as a baby, his ministry here on earth, and ultimately his death, resurrection, and return to heaven. My purpose with this book is not to spiritualize everything we see but rather to use these traditions and decorations to turn our hearts and minds toward God and to our need for a Savior.

Are we aware that many of the images we associate with Christmas reflect a pagan heritage? Yes, we are. But God himself works with unbelievers to bring them into a right relationship with him. Through his parables and other teachings, Jesus regularly used the familiar to build a bridge for understanding and accepting a "new" spiritual truth.

Do we know that many of these symbols are not at all mentioned in the Scriptures? Of course we do. We also know, from Deuteronomy 6, that we are to teach the truth and the commandments of God to our children when we are at home and when we are away, when we lie down and when we rise. We are to use what they see and hear to turn their attention to God. Is there a better gift we can give our children than to develop their ability to discover God's message of love and grace in everything around them?

With this book, I want to give you ideas that can be applied throughout the year. In all of life—not just in December—we want to encourage a continual awareness of God in ourselves and in our children, an appreciation for his work of creation and redemption and for his willingness to meet us where we are. Then we can share this wonderful news with those in our midst who are unaware of it.

This book may be useful for persons of all ages, designed as a parent-led reading time. With very young children who may not understand the deeper concepts written here, you, as the parent, may want to offer a simple summary of how a particular decoration or Christmas tradition points us to our Savior. Older children will understand at a deeper level and be able to engage with this book as you discuss it with them.

At the end of each day's reading, I have included a "Digging Deeper" section with a list of relevant Scripture verses. You may use these to extend the reading into a family Bible study. As you study God's Word together, you can discuss the lesson within the Bible passage, how it relates to the Advent reading, and contemplate how the decoration or tradition at hand can be a reminder of how God draws us nearer to himself.

Finally, on the last pages, we have provided miniature versions of the illustrations that accompany each day's reading. These are designed to be cut out and pasted onto precut wooden ornaments or tags. These tags can then be used as an Advent calendar and hung as decorations on your tree, giving a tangible reminder of each day's lesson as the month progresses.

More than anything, my hope is that, through this book, you and your family will come to know more deeply our Lord and Savior—the One whose advent we are celebrating.

May God bless your time together and your time with him this Christmas season!

December 1

The Evergreen: Christ's Death, Burial, and Resurrection

We were buried therefore with him by baptism into death, in order that, just as Christ was raised from the dead by the glory of the Father, we too might walk in newness of life.

ROMANS 6:4

*I*n many ways, the evergreen tree is the showpiece of Christmas décor, whether in the form of a Christmas tree, a Christmas wreath, or the evergreen boughs and garlands that are so prevalent. It is also the perfect starting point for our journey because the point at the top of the evergreen tree directs our thoughts heavenward.

The entirety of Scripture points us to Christ, and throughout Scripture we see the recurring image of a tree leading us forward in God's plan. The Christmas tree, then, is a representation of the many trees referenced in Scripture that prompt us to tell God's story of redemption from beginning to end—from the Tree of Life in Genesis 2 to the Tree of Life in Revelation 22. The central tree of Scripture, however, is the cross on which Jesus died to give us new life.

The Christmas tree, whether chosen from the forest or a local tree lot, has been cut down. We bring it home, set it up, and decorate it. This is a vivid picture of Christ's death (cut down), his resurrection (raised up), and his being showered with glory and honor (decorated) upon his return to heaven. It also reminds us of what happens at salvation: we die to sin, are raised to new life in Christ, and have the assurance of a future resurrection to eternal life with Christ in heaven where we have stored up spiritual treasures during our life on earth (Matthew 6:19–20).

Digging Deeper:
Genesis 2:15–3:24; Isaiah 11:1; Acts 10:34–43; Hebrews 2:6–9; Revelation 22:1–2.

December 2
Red and Green: Abundant, Everlasting Life

The thief comes only to steal and kill and destroy. I came that they may have life and have it abundantly.

JOHN 10:10

How can something as common, familiar, and simple as the traditional red and green colors of Christmas focus our attention on the child in the manger? When we bring together the ideas that Christ came in order to become the ultimate sacrifice for sin and that his sacrifice provides a way for new life, we have an ever-present object lesson in the reds and greens we see around us.

Red brings to mind the blood Christ shed for us. The abundance of this color during the Christmas season is significant because Christ did not simply spill a few drops of his blood but poured it all out for us, holding nothing back. Green represents living things and new life.

The red and green colors together remind us that the suffering and sacrifice of Christ have generated new, eternal life for us with our heavenly Father. This new life is made possible only through Christ's sacrifice. In gratitude and worship we present ourselves as a living sacrifice to Christ (Romans 12:1–2).

The poinsettia, that quintessential Christmas flower, displays these two prominent colors beautifully. The shape of this red flower, similar to a star, reminds us that Christ came to earth as a human baby, while the richness of the greens reminds us of the eternal life we have in Christ and of how abundant and deep it is.

Digging Deeper:
Matthew 26:26–29; Mark 14:22–24; John 3:1–21; Acts 13:44–52.

December 3

Holly: The Way, the Truth, and the Life

I am the way, and the truth, and the life. No one comes to the Father except through me.
JOHN 14:6

Holly is another universal Christmas decoration. It is found printed on Christmas cards, stationery, and wrapping paper. Holly leaves and berries set Christmas dishware apart. Holly adorns table centerpieces and decorates ornaments both small and large. What significance does holly hold? Is there more to be found in this beautiful plant than the simple Christmas colors?

The holly's sharp, pointed leaves are reminiscent of the thorny crown that was placed on Jesus's head before his crucifixion. That is why the plant is also known as the "Christ thorn." The bright red berries represent the blood those thorns caused to flow as Jesus chose to submit to the humiliation and curse of the cross and the mockery of those who tortured and crucified him. He did all this for us. He took the punishment for our sins (Isaiah 53:4–5). His cross is the bridge that will lead us once again into the presence of God.

In heraldry, holly leaves have long been understood as a symbol of truth. Christ called himself the way, the truth, and the life. As his ambassadors on earth, we are called to follow his example and live so others can come to know Christ by seeing us walk with him, hearing us speak the truth about him, and watching us live a Christ-honoring life.

Digging Deeper:
Matthew 27:27–31; John 19:1–16; 2 Corinthians 5:20–21; Philippians 2:1–11.

December 4

Mistletoe: Abiding in Christ

Every branch in me that does not bear fruit he takes away, and every branch
that does bear fruit he prunes, that it may bear more fruit.

JOHN 15:2

Mistletoe grows on the branches or trunk of a tree. The roots of this parasitic plant penetrate the tree and absorb its nutrients. Mistletoe must be connected to a host tree for survival. In the same way, we must be connected to Christ in order to live and bear fruit. We can have life only by being grafted into his life-giving root (Romans 11:17–24).

Once believed to have mystical powers, mistletoe was hung above doors to keep evil spirits away. It was, therefore, a sign of friendship, welcome, and safety. For a while, Christians hung mistletoe on the doors of their churches as a welcome sign, a symbol of the love and safety that could be found within. Over the years, this use faded out, and we are now left with the mere tradition of kissing under the mistletoe. Quite possibly, this tradition stems from the cultural traditions of greeting each other with a kiss of welcome, a practice mentioned in a number of Paul's epistles, rather than the romantic feelings we associate it with today.

Are those who use the tradition to steal a kiss beneath the mistletoe hoping to find true love? Probably not, but our world is desperate for love and acceptance. Maybe it's time to update this tradition in order to reach our contemporaries. Let's make sure that our homes and churches are filled with true love—the love of Christ that welcomes all who come through the door.

Digging Deeper:

John 13:34–35, 15:1–17; Romans 16:16; 1 Corinthians 13; 2 Corinthians 13:12; 1 Thessalonians 5:26.

December 5

Wreath: Eternal Joy

So also you have sorrow now, but I will see you again, and your hearts will rejoice, and no one will take your joy from you.
JOHN 16:22

In ancient times, branches and leaves of the laurel tree were twisted or "writhed" together to create crowns for kings, military heroes, and athletes. Wreaths could indicate a person's occupation, rank, achievements, or status. It was a symbol of victory, honor, or celebration, worn by returning heroes, guests at a feast, and brides at their wedding.

Our Savior wore a crown of thorns, wound together by Roman soldiers in order to mock the man they were ordered to crucify. When Jesus returns to earth, however, he will come as the glorious, invincible King, wearing many crowns.

It is hard to say how the wreath transformed from a crown to be worn into a decoration to hang on our doors. It may be that the person who received the crown hung it when the time for wearing it came to an end, much like we might dry and preserve a bouquet of flowers. Maybe wreaths were hung on homes as a symbol that the inhabitants were rejoicing over some event. However it came about, the Christmas wreath continues to represent victory, honor, and celebration of a glorious event—Christ's victory over sin and death, honor for the King of kings, and celebration of the hope of eternal joy in the presence of a loving God.

Digging Deeper:
Isaiah 28:5–6, 62:3; Matthew 27:27–31; 1 Corinthians 9:24–27; 2 Timothy 4:6–8; Hebrews 2:5–9; 1 Peter 5:4; Revelation 3:11–13, 19:11–13.

December 6

Saint Nicholas: Giving as an Act of Worship

When you give to the needy, do not let your left hand know what your right hand is doing, so that your giving may be in secret. And your Father who sees in secret will reward you.

MATTHEW 6:3–4

Saint Nicholas was the bishop of Myra in the fourth century and is remembered for his generosity to the poor and needy. The thoughtful deeds attributed to him were all done in secret. He exemplified the words of Jesus which call us to the type of giving that is between only ourselves and our heavenly Father (Matthew 6:3–4). This giving is characterized by the selfless desire to bless another, with no thought or expectation for what we may get in return.

In today's depictions of St. Nick, the bishop's miter and fur-trimmed garments of old have morphed into Santa's characteristic red suit, and the man has become a fairytale figure with magical powers. The real Saint Nicholas stood out as a kind man with an eye for practical needs, with a heartfelt love for the poor and disadvantaged, and with a humble attitude. These are characteristics we can imitate. Like him, let us keep our eyes and hearts open to those whom the Lord brings into our lives. Let us be generous in alleviating needs, building up with encouraging words, and praying fervently for others.

In its simplest form, giving is an act of worship. God is honored when we do so graciously and for the right reasons.

Digging Deeper:
Proverbs 14:31; 2 Corinthians 9:6–15; 1 Timothy 6:17–19; James 2:14–26; 1 John 3:16–18.

December 7

Reindeer: The Rejected Cornerstone

The stone that the builders rejected has become the cornerstone.

PSALM 118:22

The poem, "'Twas the Night Before Christmas," published anonymously in 1823, is the basis for most of today's understanding of Saint Nicholas/Santa Claus. Along with a detailed description of St. Nick himself, the author also introduced "eight tiny rein-deer" to his lore. It wasn't until 1939, however, that Santa's ninth reindeer, Rudolph, was introduced. With that introduction, we not only gain a cute story, but these reindeer figures also give us another connection to a spiritual truth.

Rudolph's shiny nose made him an outcast among his fellow reindeer—until that fateful foggy Christmas Eve when Santa chose him to guide the sleigh on its journey. Despite his earlier rejection, Rudolph returned that night a hero. In fact, he "went down in history" as the one who saved Christmas for the world by lighting the way.

In many ways, Jesus was also an outcast. He came into this world as a poor boy. His own people should have recognized him, yet they rejected and scorned him. Jesus is the only One who can provide the light the world needs, and he is the only One who can show the way to salvation. Only Jesus Christ can save. Without him, we are stuck in the thick, dense fog of a sinful life.

Do we find ourselves in the position of the "normal" reindeer? Do we scorn the only One who can bring salvation—Jesus, our cornerstone? As his followers, let us become living stones and part of the house of God (1 Peter 2:1–12).

Digging Deeper:
Matthew 13:53–58; Mark 6:1–6; 1 Corinthians 1:26–31; James 4:6.

December 8

Stocking: The Rewarding Journey

Well done, good and faithful servant. You have been faithful over a little; I will
set you over much. Enter into the joy of your master.
MATTHEW 25:21

*I*n the fourth century, stockings were hung by the fireplace to dry overnight. When Saint Nicholas—according to the legend—tossed a girl's dowry through the window one night, the gift landed in her stocking, where she discovered it the next morning.

In German and Dutch folklore, we find Saint Nicholas putting special gifts in shoes or stockings left out for him by children. By the sixteenth century, a twist to the story emerged that had St. Nick punishing naughty girls and boys by leaving lumps of coal in place of the desired gift.

Even this folklore can provide an object lesson to remind us of God's plan for his children. In 1 Corinthians 3, Paul describes two types of believers. The first believer lives a life marked by selfless love as he seeks to bring honor to his Savior. Like the good child, this person receives a reward when their deeds survive the Refiner's fire. The second type of believer is the one whose deeds in this life are marked by selfish ambition. These will not survive the refining fires, and the result is like the disappointing lump of coal. On the day that we enter heaven, will our deeds of this life survive the Refiner's fire?

Digging Deeper:
Matthew 25:14–46; Luke 19:11–27; 1 Corinthians 3:10–15; 2 Timothy 4:6–8.

December 9

Sleigh: The Threshing Floor

His winnowing fork is in his hand, and he will clear his threshing floor and gather his
wheat into the barn, but the chaff he will burn with unquenchable fire.

MATTHEW 3:12

The sleighs we most associate with Christmas are the one horse open sleigh and the classic toy sled that boys and girls might find under the Christmas tree. When we broaden our understanding of the sleigh, however, we once again find a beautiful connection to God's Word and another object lesson that shows us God is always speaking to our hearts if we have the ears to hear.

Before the age of combine harvesters, another type of sleigh—also called a sled or sledge—was used in the threshing and winnowing of grain. The broad, flat bottom of a heavy platform-style sled was fitted with teeth that, when pulled over the grain on the threshing floor, crushed and cut and separated the chaff (the husks and stalks that have no value) from the grain, the valuable seed. This method of threshing grain, mentioned in Job and Isaiah, would have been commonly understood to the people of Jesus's day. What Jesus says in Matthew 3:12 about separating the wheat from the chaff would have been a very clear word picture for his audience. At the end of this age, Jesus Christ will clear his threshing floor to separate the wheat from the chaff. The repentant believer in Christ will be gathered into his Father's house, while those who have rejected Christ and the gift of salvation that he offers will in turn be rejected by the Father. Let us accept God's wonderful gift of Christ this season!

Digging Deeper:
Job 41:30; Psalm 1:4; Isaiah 28:27–28, 41:15–16; Matthew 3:1–12; Luke 3:15–20.

December 10

Bells: A Proclamation

Go therefore and make disciples of all nations, baptizing them in the name of the Father and of the Son and of the Holy Spirit, teaching them to observe all that I have commanded you. And behold, I am with you always, to the end of the age.

MATTHEW 28:19–20

Bells seem to have a natural connection to Christmas. Sleigh bells warn of the approach of a winter carriage that otherwise glides quietly over the snow, and church bells announce the beginning of Christmas services. *It's a Wonderful Life*, the classic Christmas movie, claims that the ringing of a bell announces that an angel has earned his wings.

In general, bells are rung to call attention to an upcoming event, an imminent announcement, or a proclamation. American tradition tells us the Liberty Bell sounded just before the first public reading of the Declaration of Independence. A school bell announces the commencement of class, wedding bells announce the beginning of a new marriage, and doorbells announce the presence of guests.

What spiritual lesson can we glean from Christmas bells? In biblical times, the high priest wore bells on the hem of his robe to announce his coming and going in the holy place. The responsibility of the high priest was to be a mediator between God and his people. Jesus came to earth to fulfill many different roles, including being our eternal High Priest. In this role, Jesus becomes the mediator between God and his people, providing a way for us to have direct access once again to our heavenly Father. Christmas bells proclaim the celebration of the birth of the Messiah, our eternal High Priest. We know the way, the truth, and the life, and we must proclaim him to the world.

Digging Deeper:
Exodus 28:31–35; Zechariah 14:20; Romans 10:14–17; Hebrews 7:11–28.

December 11

Ornaments: A Precious Life in the Hands of the Master

You formed my inward parts; you knitted me together in my mother's womb.

PSALM 139:13

The variety of ways different families decorate their Christmas trees is fascinating. Some families choose ornaments that are unified in color and style, giving their tree a beautiful, elegant, and refined appearance. Others choose to use ornaments of varied origin and style, giving their tree a comfortable, homespun charm. No matter how we choose to decorate our Christmas tree, it gives the viewer a glimpse into the character of our family. But our ornaments can also tell another story.

We carefully pack our valued ornaments and store them from year to year. They are often fragile or carry special meaning, so we handle them with care. We put them out of the reach of little hands or curious pets. The delicacy of these ornaments can be a reminder of how fragile this life is and why we should depend on God alone for everything.

Many ornaments are carefully crafted—some by loving little hands, others by talented craftsmen—and bring to mind the story of the potter who shapes his vessels with great care (Isaiah 64:8). He has a special purpose in mind for each article he works on. Likewise, our heavenly Father shapes you and me with utmost attention to detail for his purposes. Our aim should be to remain as malleable vessels in the hands of the divine potter. Only in becoming the person he made us to be will we find satisfaction and contentment.

Digging Deeper:
Psalm 139:13–16; Isaiah 29:15–16, 45:9; Jeremiah 18:1–11; Romans 9:19–21; 2 Timothy 2:20–21.

December 12

Candy Cane: Christ's Body Broken for Us

This is my body, which is given for you. Do this in remembrance of me.
LUKE 22:19

The candy cane is probably the most recognized Christmas treat and is rich with reminders of Christ. It is shaped like a shepherd's crook and, when turned on end, looks like the letter J. This reminds us that Jesus is the Good Shepherd.

The original candy cane has red and white stripes. The three thin red stripes represent the three instances during which Christ shed blood before the crucifixion: during his prayer in the garden of Gethsemane, during his flogging in the midst of his trial, and when the crown of thorns was pressed down upon his head. The thicker red stripe speaks to the blood Jesus shed on the cross. The red stripes of the candy cane are on a white background, indicating that when the blood of Christ washes over us in the forgiveness of sin, we are made as white as newly fallen snow (Isaiah 1:18).

The traditional candy cane bursts with a fresh, minty flavor, too, which can remind us that our new life in Christ is a fresh start: "The old has passed away; behold, the new has come" (2 Corinthians 5:17).

Candy canes are delicate and break easily. It is difficult to keep them whole. We can turn our disappointment over the broken pieces into praise and thanksgiving when we remember that Christ's body was broken for us (1 Corinthians 11:23–26 NKJV). That is the good news of the gospel that we share.

Digging Deeper:
Isaiah 53; Matthew 27:27–31; Luke 18:31–33, 22:39–46; John 10:1–18, 19:1–37; 2 Corinthians 5:16–21.

December 13

Candles: The Light of the World

I am the light of the world. Whoever follows me will not walk in darkness, but will have the light of life.
JOHN 8:12

Some countries and some denominations celebrate Santa Lucia Day on December 13. This celebration once coincided with the winter solstice and became known as the Festival of Light. According to legend, Lucia was martyred for her faith in the fourth century because she would take baskets of food to Christians hiding in the catacombs of Rome. Since these underground cemeteries were dark, she wore a wreath of candles on her head to light her way, leaving her hands free to carry the provisions.

Traditionally, candles were used to light homes and decorate Christmas trees until they were replaced by multicolored electric lights. Many people put up elaborate light displays during this season, even those who do not know the Light of the World, whose birth we are celebrating. This Christmas, let's show everyone we meet that we are followers of Jesus. Let's share with them the good news of salvation through God's Son, Jesus. The world will become a brighter place with more worshippers of the one and only true God.

Even in the darkest times, we know where to find light. Jesus is the light that leads us to salvation, and he remains our light as we journey to heaven. He brings light to the darkest places we might wander; he never leaves us.

Digging Deeper:
Psalm 23:4; Isaiah 42:6–7, 60:1; Micah 7:7–8; Matthew 4:15–16, 5:13–16; Luke 1:76–79; John 1:1–13.

December 14

Gingerbread: A Firm Foundation

Everyone then who hears these words of mine and does them will be like a wise man who built his house on the rock.
MATTHEW 7:24

The gingerbread man is a common Christmas treat found on many holiday cookie platters. This cute little character did not create itself; it is the creation of a baker. This is a reminder that we, too, have been created by a loving God. We are his possession, created to worship him, but we strayed, choosing instead a life of sinful rebellion against him. Christmas is all about God's endeavor to redeem us to himself through the sacrifice of his Son.

The gingerbread house is another popular decoration this time of year. After all, our little gingerbread man needs a home! There are gingerbread house parties and even competitions where the central event is building and decorating these edible concoctions. In this context, we can call to mind the parable Jesus told of the two men who built themselves new houses. The foolish man built his house on the sand, taking the easy path. The wise man recognized the folly of this unstable foundation and chose instead to build his house on a rock.

The world's answers to life's problems are shouting out to us everywhere—at school, in the workplace, even through the television in our own home. It is the wise man who recognizes the folly of building his life to the world's standards. We must build our lives instead on the firm foundation of Christ, the only foundation we can trust.

Digging Deeper:
Genesis 1:26–31; Matthew 7:24–29; 1 Corinthians 3:10–15.

December 15

Yule Log: Certainty of Christ's Return

And if I go and prepare a place for you, I will come again and will take you to myself, that where I am you may be also.
JOHN 14:3

There are many traditions and superstitions connected with the burning of the yule log. The origins probably go back to the pagan rite of sun worshippers who celebrated the return of the sun after the winter solstice, when the days began to lengthen. They wanted to honor the unconquered sun god.

We can view this celebration from a Christian perspective. Instead of sun worshippers, we are Son worshippers who, during yuletide, celebrate the unconquered Son of God. Christ came as a baby—fully God and fully man—to identify with us, his creation. He grew up and stood firm in the face of every temptation. In so doing, he lived a sinless and holy life. When he died on the cross, he took upon himself the punishment for the sins of the entire world, providing redemption to all who trust in him. He was buried but rose again. He returned to heaven but promises that he will one day return to earth in final victory. Though Christ died, he conquered death in his resurrection; though his heel was bruised, he crushed the enemy's head. He is truly the unconquered conqueror!

If you burn a yule log during the Christmas season, don't let it be a meaningless tradition. Let's remember who we celebrate and why. Burn a yule log in celebration of Christ's return, which will most certainly take place in God's appointed time.

Digging Deeper:
Genesis 3:15; John 14:1–6; 1 Thessalonians 4:13–18; Revelation 11:15, 17:14.

December 16

Christmas Carols: A Heart of Worship

I will sing of the steadfast love of the LORD, forever; with my mouth I will make known your faithfulness to all generations.
PSALM 89:1

Have you ever noticed the effect that certain Christmas carols have on your mood, your step, or your actions? When we hear certain songs, we can't help but sing along or smile and greet strangers in a way that we wouldn't any other time of year. Christmas carols, secular or religious, have a way of putting us in the Christmas spirit, which is an attitude of celebration.

The lyrics of many Christmas carols convey the real meaning of the holiday. They clearly express that Christmas celebrates our Savior's coming to earth. Christmas is also a time when Christians anticipate Christ's second coming.

Over and over, the Bible invites us to sing—sing to the Lord, come into God's presence with singing, sing a new song, sing joyfully. There are many examples in the Bible of people worshipping God through song. In Exodus, we read of Miriam singing a song of thanksgiving. The Psalms are a collection of songs written for the worship of God. In the gospel according to Luke, we find Mary singing to God when she learns that she has been chosen to bear his Son. In Revelation, we read of songs that are sung in heaven. Singing is a natural part of worship; in fact, today we often equate the two. Let us sing with hearts and minds focused on the One worthy of our worship.

Digging Deeper:
Exodus 15:21; 1 Chronicles 16:23–25; Psalm 100; Isaiah 42:10–13, 49:13; Luke 1:46–56; Revelation 5:9–14, 15:1–4.

December 17

Snowflakes: Precious and Valued in the Kingdom

God arranged the members in the body, each one of them, as he chose.
1 CORINTHIANS 12:18

The scientific consensus is that no two snow crystals are exactly alike in molecular structure or appearance. The water droplets that become ice crystals vary widely from one another. The newly formed crystals are sensitive to atmospheric conditions and change in response to them. Alone, each tiny snowflake is uniquely beautiful, but together, they create magnificent winter scenes that awe and inspire us.

Like the snowflakes, every single human being is unique. And each one of us is beautiful because we are created in the image of God and knit together in our mother's womb. We are made with a special purpose and given specific talents and gifts. Human life, from its very first moment, is infinitely precious and valuable. Every person created has eternal value and a unique part in God's plan.

Just as a gathering of snowflakes can make a difference to a landscape, so Christians can make a difference where they are. Like a beautiful landscape, others recognize God's handiwork when his people use their God-given gifts to love one another. When this love is put into action, God is glorified and the community of peoples are blessed.

Digging Deeper:
Job 10:11–12; Psalm 139:13–16; John 13:31–35; 1 Corinthians 12:12–31.

December 18

Snowman: A Softened Heart

And I will give you a new heart, and a new spirit I will put within you. And I will remove the heart of stone from your flesh and give you a heart of flesh.

Ezekiel 36:26

Where there is snow, there is bound to be a snowman sooner or later. "Frosty the Snowman" was popularized with the hit song by Gene Autry in 1950, but many of us are also familiar with the 1969 Rankin/Bass animated children's classic by the same name. In this cartoon version, Frosty selflessly sacrifices himself for the sake of a little girl named Karen by melting into a puddle of water. This provides a very simplified picture of Christ's example of sacrificial love for us, which we are also called to show one another (John 15:12–13).

The snowman is a figure of humanity. Just as the snowman will melt in the heat of the sun, so our cold and frozen hearts, hardened in the grip of sin, can melt when exposed to the love of Christ. As we begin to grasp just how deeply he loves us and what a steep price he paid to free us from the bondage of sin, our hearts soften, and our eyes turn toward him.

How do we know that we have hardened hearts in need of a little melting? There are several indicators of a hardened heart, such as fear, pride, and unforgiveness. These elements, if left unchecked, will turn our hearts as cold and hard as ice. On the other hand, if we trust God, love others selflessly, and forgive them readily, we can experience hearts softened by the power of Christ.

Digging Deeper:
John 8:34–38, 15:12–17; Ephesians 4:17–24; 1 John 3:16–24.

December 19

Angels: Fear Not

Fear not, for behold, I bring you good news of great joy that will be for all the people.
LUKE 2:10

Many families top their Christmas tree with an angel. Angels appear multiple times in the Christmas story, so this connection is fairly well understood. We hear of an angel appearing to Mary and later to Joseph, telling them of the coming of Christ and their roles in that event. At the birth of Christ, a multitude of angels appear to the shepherds at Bethlehem, telling them the joyous news of the birth of the Messiah. Later, an angel warns Joseph of King Herod's plan to murder the child Jesus and tells him to move to Egypt.

Angels, servants of God in the unseen world, are referenced throughout Scripture. Angels battle invisible enemy forces to defend God's people. They are messengers of encouragement, destruction, protection, and prophecy according to God's command. The words "Fear not," or some variation thereof, often precede the message the angel brings.

However, these are not the only times in God's Word that we hear this message. God knows our fearful hearts and often reassures us with promises like "It is the LORD who goes before you. He will be with you; he will not leave you or forsake you. Do not fear or be dismayed" (Deuteronomy 31:8). When we have a healthy fear and understanding of God based on respect and honor, we have no need to fear the world or our circumstances.

Digging Deeper:

Genesis 21:1–21; Joshua 8:1–2; Daniel 10:8–19; Matthew 1:18–24, 2:13–15, 10:26–33, 28:1–10; Luke 1:1–38, 2:8–20; Acts 27:21–26; Hebrews 13:5–6.

December 20

Shepherd: In Jesus's Care

I am the good shepherd. The good shepherd lays down his life for the sheep.
JOHN 10:11

A shepherd's job is to care for the sheep. The shepherd travels with his flock, spending day and night with the sheep, guiding them to pasture and water, and keeping them safe. Because he essentially shares life with his sheep, the shepherd naturally collects the dirt and grime of the outdoors, the smell of the sheep, and the perspiration that comes from his work. He lives a lonely life not only because of his constant and intimate involvement with the flock but also because society does not regard shepherds highly.

Despite their lowly status, shepherds were the first to hear the good news of the birth of the long-awaited Messiah who came to die for sinners. God acknowledged them, and he identified with them. Jesus described himself as the Good Shepherd because he is always with us. He guides us through storms and shares our griefs and joys. We are never alone. The Good Shepherd uses his rod and staff to stop us from running away and getting lost. He walks with us, guides us, and will rescue us from the eternal consequences of our sin if we let him. Even if our earthly bodies experience sickness and harm, the Good Shepherd will work all things together for the good of those who love him and are called according to his purpose (Romans 8:28).

Digging Deeper:
Isaiah 40:11; Ezekiel 34; Psalm 23; Luke 2:8–20; John 10:1–21.

December 21

Lamb: God's Wrath Passes Over

Behold, the Lamb of God, who takes away the sin of the world!
JOHN 1:29

Nativities often include sheep and lambs. The story of the first Christmas night tells us about shepherds tending their sheep, and we assume the presence of animals in the stable where Jesus was born. Sheep were very important animals in Hebrew worship, for the blood of their sacrifice covered the sins of the people.

The story of the exodus introduces us to the Passover lamb. Each family had to procure a perfect lamb and take care of it for four days—possibly falling in love with it—before it was slaughtered. They painted their doorposts and lintels with its blood. This was a sign to the Angel of Death to pass over that home when he came in judgment on all those in Egypt, because a lamb had died in the place of the firstborn son of that family. The lamb's blood pointed to the suffering of the promised Deliverer. When Jesus revealed himself as the Messiah to the Jews, he made it clear that he had not come to conquer the Romans or free God's people from their earthly overlords. Rather, he had come to conquer spiritual death, for the wages of sin is death (Romans 6:23), and to free all who believed in him from enslavement to their sinful nature.

Not only is Jesus the Good Shepherd, but he is also the sacrificial Lamb of God who takes away the sin of the world. Christ died in our place so the wrath of God could pass over us—because we put ourselves under the blood of the Lamb through repentance.

Digging Deeper:
Exodus 12:1–28; John 1:29–34; Romans 6:15–23; Revelation 5.

December 22

Kings: Perfect Authority

They will make war on the Lamb, and the Lamb will conquer them, for he is Lord of lords and King of kings, and those with him are called and chosen and faithful.

REVELATION 17:14

The nativity story includes the local shepherds, people of very little esteem, but it also includes kings or foreign wisemen, people who were powerful and of high estate. This shows us that Christ came as the Savior for all people—rich and poor, Jew and Gentile, slave and free, male and female.

In addition to being our High Priest and the Good Shepherd, Jesus is also the King of kings. He is the only One who has absolute and complete authority. He has authority over nature as demonstrated when he calms a storm (Matthew 8:23–27). The apostle Peter tells us Christ is given authority over both the angels and the rulers of the world (1 Peter 3:21–22.) Throughout his ministry on earth, Jesus frequently demonstrates his authority over Satan and his demons. Jesus is also the holy Lamb of God and, thus, is the only One who has authority to forgive sins.

His authority is not only perfect in the sense of completeness but also in the sense of purity. Jesus is one with the Father and, therefore, perfect and holy in every way, including his authority. He is the One through whom all things are created and sustained. He is superior to the angels and the head of the church. All things belong to him. What an honor it is to be a part of his kingdom!

Digging Deeper:
Matthew 2:1–12; Mark 2:1–12, 4:35–41; Luke 4:31–37, 5:17–26; John 5:19–29, 19:1–16; Colossians 1:15–20; Hebrews 1.

December 23

Stars: Watch and Respond

Where is he who has been born king of the Jews? For we saw his star when it rose and have come to worship him.

MATTHEW 2:2

Stars! You can't have Christmas decorations without finding a star somewhere—stars on the treetops; stars on the housetops; stars on the hilltops, the skyscrapers, and the jib arms of cranes. Just look, stars are gleaming everywhere!

The star belongs to the biblical Christmas story yet still remains relatively free of controversy. We can use this ever-present visual aid to talk about God's wonderful plan of salvation. The stars we see can remind us of the star that guided the God-fearing magi of the east to Bethlehem to honor the newborn king of the Jews. These men were probably familiar with the prophecies of Daniel. They were highly educated in astronomy and observed the skies. This knowledge allowed them to recognize the movement of the hand of God and respond to it by traveling to Judea.

We can follow the example of the magi in our lives. We should study the Scriptures to know God's plan, recognize his work around us, and respond to his leading. We are told in Luke 21:25–28 that there will be signs in the heavens and the earth that will precede Christ's return. Like the magi of old, we should be watching and ready for his second advent. And as we are challenged in 1 Peter 3:15, we should be ready with an answer for anyone who asks for a reason for the hope that we have.

Digging Deeper:
Isaiah 60:1–6; Matthew 2:1–12; Mark 13:32–37; 2 Timothy 4:1–5; Titus 2:11–15.

December 24

Gifts: Joy in Both Giving and Receiving

For the wages of sin is death, but the free gift of God is eternal life in Christ Jesus our Lord.
ROMANS 6:23

It is a joy to give and receive gifts. At Christmas, we celebrate the arrival of the most amazing gift: Jesus Christ, the eternal Son of God who became a man in order to bring sinners back to God by purchasing them for eternal life (Revelation 5:9). The person who accepts Jesus Christ and his gift of eternal life experiences joy and peace of such magnitude it is beyond all human understanding.

The Christmas story also tells of gifts given to Jesus. When the magi came to worship the new king, they brought him gold, frankincense, and myrrh. These gifts, worthy of a king, were given to a young boy who'd been born to poor parents. The magi did not see Jesus as a baby in the manger as we often imagine, but when they found him, it was obvious he was not a typical king. Nevertheless, they believed the prophecies and the signs and, by giving Jesus these gifts, recognized him as the king they had come to honor.

During his public ministry, Jesus also used the understanding of gifts to teach his followers about the love God has for his people. He explained in Matthew 7:11 how God's holy love for his children causes him to give good and perfect gifts to them.

Whether we give or receive gifts, we hope they will bring joy and be useful. Likewise, God gives his children spiritual gifts. We find blessings and joy when we develop and use these gifts for his glory.

Digging Deeper:
Matthew 2:1–12; Luke 11:5–13; Romans 6:20–23; 1 Corinthians 12; Ephesians 4:7–13; James 1:17–18.

December 25

The Baby in the Manger: Sit at Jesus's feet

And she had a sister called Mary, who sat at the Lord's feet and listened to his teaching.
LUKE 10:39

We've all heard the Christian Christmas slogans: "Jesus is the reason for the season!"; "Keep Christ in Christmas"; "Christmas begins with Christ."

Christians and churches use these phrases throughout the month of December. But have they become cliché? Do we ever pause to internalize the thoughts they're expressing? Or do we let ourselves get caught up in the busyness of gift giving, plays, cantatas, and Christmas Eve services—or even serving the poor and needy—only to realize later that, despite our good intentions, we have become like Martha? She was so busy preparing food for her Lord and his disciples that she had no time to sit at his feet and listen to him.

For many people, Christmas Day is a very busy time, filled with many activities. Travel, family dinners and traditions, gift exchanges—all these expectations and self-imposed duties and responsibilities keep us from spending time with the One whose birthday we are supposedly celebrating.

Let's make this Christmas different. Set aside the natural tendency of Martha and follow Mary's example. Mary hung on every word Jesus said, and he was very pleased with that. Let us take time to set aside the worries, cares, and preparations so we can sit intentionally at the feet of Jesus.

Digging Deeper:
Matthew 19:13–15; Luke 5:1–3, 10:38–42, 19:1–10; Hebrews 3:1–6.

Epilogue

The Everyday Things of Life: God's Message to You

For his invisible attributes, namely, his eternal power and divine nature, have been clearly perceived, ever since the creation of the world, in the things that have been made. So they are without excuse.

ROMANS 1:20

Throughout the month of December, we have taken time each day to look around us, to see the common things of life in a new light at this time of year. We have taken time to meditate on the Word (John 1:1) and the messages that he brings—messages of love, forgiveness, salvation, and purpose. Now what? Advent and Christmas are over. Is there more? Yes!

The Word of God is so rich and deep, there is no end to the flow of living water and spiritual nourishment he provides (Romans 11:33). His love for the world is so vast that he reveals himself clearly in the world around us. As a result, he leaves no excuse for not knowing him (Romans 1:20). Are your spiritual eyes open, watching for him and the message he has for you in the everyday things of life? Would you then open his written word to you, the Bible, and verify that message?

Jesus is not only the reason for the season, he is also the reason for living from day to day (Romans 12:1). I encourage you to search him out in your daily life and to teach your children to do so too (Deuteronomy 6:6–7). Together, you are sure to find blessings beyond measure as you continue to be intentional about sitting at his feet.

Author Bio

Marissa Barbee, a long-time resident of Colorado, was raised on a ranch in eastern Oregon. She is a wife of twenty years and a home-educating mother of nine children. Marissa and her husband Scott enjoy playing games with their children and tackling projects—from the challenges of gardening in the Rockies to the DIY remodeling of their home. *Christmas Traditions through the Lens of Scripture* was born from a passion which began in 1989 after Marissa heard the story of the candy cane's origin. Following this, she watched, listened, and made connections between many Christmas traditions and her faith in Christ. You can connect with Marissa on Instagram at instagram.com/mrsmarissabarbee or on Facebook at facebook.com/mrsmarissabarbee.

Illustrator Bio

Miriam Barbee, daughter of Marissa Barbee and the oldest of nine children, is a talented artist with a passion for sharing the beauty of God's creation through her art. Miriam's signature style makes use of artistic framing to highlight the subject of her artwork and to give the viewer the sense of peering through a window or doorway into a much wider world. She uses many different mediums in her work, including pencil and oil, watercolor, and acrylic paints. You can find Miriam's art at paintinginframes.com and can connect with her on Instagram at instagram.com/painting_in_frames.

ORDER INFORMATION

To order additional copies of this book, please visit
www.redemption-press.com.
Also available on Amazon.com and BarnesandNoble.com
or by calling toll-free 1-844-2REDEEM.

Printed in the USA
CPSIA information can be obtained
at www.ICGtesting.com
LVHW070056161123
764005LV00007B/72

9 781646 456499